FOOTBALL JOKES

THE CHILD'S WORLD

Illustrated by Viki Woodworth.

Library of Congress Catalog-in-Publication Data
Rothaus, James R.
Football Jokes / Jim Rothaus
p. cm.
Summary: A collection of jokes and riddles featuring football
players, coaches, and the game in general.
ISBN 1-56766-267-6 (lib.bdg.)

1. Riddles, Juvenile. 2. Knock-knock jokes. 3. Football –
Juvenile humor. [1. Jokes. 2. Riddles. 3. Knock-knock jokes.]
I. Title
PN6371.5R678 1997   95-50119
818'.5402 — dc20   CIP
[B]   AC

FOOTBALL JOKES

Written and Compiled by James R. Rothaus
Illustrated by Viki Woodworth

What happens when you kick a football in the lake?

It gets wet. ⇨

What surface do they put down on
football fields in outer space?
Astroturf.

Knock-knock.
Who's there?
Hominy.
Hominy who?
Hominy plays did we run in that series?

Why was the quarterback expelled from
school?
Because he couldn't pass.

Knock-knock.
Who's there?
Hertz.
Hertz who?
Hertz to have that play called back.

If a fullback is worth $1.00, how much
is a halfback worth?
Fifty cents.

Where is the best place to leave your dog when you go to a football game?
In the barking lot. ⇦

If a fullback is worth $1.00, how much is a quarterback worth?
Twenty-five cents.

Knock-knock.
Who's there?
Holden.
Holden who?
Holden the ball for the kicker.

How can you keep the nose guard from smelling out the plays?
Put a plug in his nose.

Knock-knock.
Who's there?
Otto B.
Otto B. who?
Otto B. instant replay in football.

What is the most popular deodorant with football players?
Right Guard.

What football team can't find its stadium?

Raiders of the lost park. ⇨

Player: *Coach, my doctor says I can't play football.*
Coach: *I could have told you that.*

Knock-knock.
Who's there?
Luke.
Luke who?
Luke out for the screen pass.

How cold was it?
It was so cold at football practice, even the clock had to rub its hands together.

Knock-knock.
Who's there?
Ken.
Ken who?
Ken I carry the ball on the next play?

Teacher: *This essay about your cat is exactly the same as your sister's.*
Football Player: *Well, it's the same cat.*

What is the most relaxed bowl game?

The Siesta Bowl. ⇦

Quarterback: *Coach, I can't seem to remember the plays.*
Coach: *When did you first notice that?*
Quarterback: *Notice what?*

Knock-knock.
Who's there?
Juwana.
Juwana who?
Juwana play catch?

Don: *My girlfriend said she would be true to the end.*
George: *What's wrong with that?*
Don: *I'm a fullback.*

Knock-knock.
Who's there?
Stan.
Stan who?
Stan back and I'll throw you a pass.

Sign in coach's office: *Exercise and diet are the best ways to fight hazardous waists.*

What did the scale say to the overweight football player?

One person at a time. ⇨

Positive pep talk by coach: *All right, team, here we are unbeaten, untied and unscored upon and ready for the first game of the season.*

Knock-knock.
Who's there?
Snow.
Snow who?
Snow use crying over a bad call.

In an NFL trade by the Chargers,
They received a player named Rodgers.
In this mixed up ordeal,
Made by "Let's Make A Deal",
He ended up with the Los Angeles
Dodgers.

Knock-knock.
Who's there?
Titus.
Titus who?
Titus string around your finger so you won't forget the play.

Coach: *What would go well with our new striped socks?*
Players: *Hip boots.* ⬅

Negative pep talk by coach: *Okay, team, if we kick off, block the try for point. If we receive, be sure and recover the fumble.*

Knock-knock.
Who's there?
Watt.
Watt who?
Watt a difference a play makes.

How hot was it?
It was so hot at football practice today, we took turns sitting in each others shadows.

There once was a player named Clyde,
Who was called for being off side.
When asked by the coach,
What caused him to encroach?
"Poor timing, I guess," he replied.

Knock-knock.
Who's there?
Shirley M.
Shirley M. who?
Shirley M. glad you caught the pass.

Why do some kickers wear two different shoes?

So they can remember which foot to kick with. ⇨

When does a lineman become two players?
When he is beside himself.

Knock-knock.
Who's there?
Fenner.
Fenner who?
Fenner you going to call my play?

There once was a coach from Purdue,
Who's team always wore the right shoe.
But he was kind of a klutz,
Who wore Nikes with his tux,
And patten leathers with cleats in
them, too.

Knock-knock.
Who's there?
Ben.
Ben who?
Ben over and hike the ball.

Why did the football player eat firecrackers?

So his hair would come out in bangs. ⟵

Coach to kicker: *Go in there and kick a field goal.*
Kicker: *I can't, my foot is asleep.*

Knock-knock.
Who's there?
Bob.
Bob who?
Bob over and hike it again.

The Raiders team owner, Al Davis,
Moves teams faster than Hertz, Budget or Avis.
In the last words he has spoken,
They're returning to Oakland.
Where the Raiders became world famous.

Knock-knock.
Who's there?
Kick-off.
Kick-off who?
Kick-off your shoes and relax.

How does a cheerleader like her hamburger?

Rah. ⇨

What does an invisible football player drink?
Evaporated Gatorade.

Knock-knock.
Who's there?
Alex.
Alex who?
Alex plain the play later.

There was a young lady named Sue,
Who was part of the cheerleading crew.
She cheered, oh, so badly,
I thought she would gladly,
Have stopped long before she was through.

Knock-knock.
Who's there?
Dewey.
Dewey who?
Dewey go for six or kick a field goal?

What football player wears the biggest helmet?

The one with the biggest head. ⇦

There are two sides to every football penalty unless you are personally involved; in which case there is only one.

Knock-knock.
Who's there?
Emmerson.
Emmerson who?
Emmerson nice football shoes you're wearing.

A young rookie drafted by Green Bay,
Wanted ever so badly to play.
When they posted the roster,
There was Smith, Jones and Foster,
But no rookie named Patrick O'Shea.

Knock-knock.
Who's there?
Hackett.
Hackett who?
I can't Hackett anymore.